# ANCESTRY AND KINDRED

.. OF ..

# W. P. ZUBER,

TEXAS VETERAN.

Windham Press is committed to bringing the lost cultural heritage of ages past into the 21st century through high-quality reproductions of original, classic printed works at affordable prices.

This book has been carefully crafted to utilize the original images of antique books rather than error-prone OCR text. This also preserves the work of the original typesetters of these classics, unknown craftsmen who laid out the text, often by hand, of each and every page you will read. Their subtle art involving judgment and interaction with the text is in many ways superior and more human than the mechanical methods utilized today, and gave each book a unique, hand-crafted feel in its text that connected the reader organically to the art of bindery and book-making.

We think these benefits are worth the occasional imperfection resulting from the age of these books at the time of scanning, and their vintage feel provides a connection to the past that goes beyond the mere words of the text.

As bibliophiles, we are always seeking perfection in our work, so please notify us of any errors in this book by emailing us at corrections@windhampress.com. Our team is motivated to correct errors quickly so future customers are better served. Our mission is to raise the bar of quality for reprinted works by a focus on detail and quality over mass production.

To peruse our catalog of carefully curated classic works, please visit our online store at www.windhampress.com.

WINDHAM PRESS
CLASSIC REPRINTS

# ANCESTRY AND KINDRED

.. OF ..

# W. P. ZUBER,

TEXAS VETERAN.

# DEDICATION.

---

*To My Near Relatives and Personal Friends:*

This little book is a delineation of my ancestry on all lines, so far as I can trace it. So far as I know, none of my progenitors have ever held high official stations: and hence I do not deem the book interesting to the public. But, so far as my knowledge extends, most of them have faithfully performed their respective duties to their families, their neighbors, their country and their God: therefore their examples are worthy of emulation, and they are as honorable as if they had filled the highest positions to which men could elevate them; and, to their descendants, their memory ought to be no less precious. To those of their descendants whom I know, and to those whose personal friendship for us may cause them to feel interest in it, this little volume is affectionately presented.

W. P. ZUBER.

Iola, Texas, July, 1905.

# ANCESTRY AND KINDRED

OF

# W. P. ZUBER, TEXAS VETERAN.

Tracing my ancestry, I give precedence to the female lines; that, when I reach any male ancestor, I may adhere to the male line so far as it points toward myself: and I mention my female ancestors by their maiden names.

I, William Physick Zuber, was born in Twiggs County, Georgia; July 6, 1820. My parents were Abraham Zuber jr. and Mary Ann Mann.

My mother, Mary Ann Mann, was born in Edgefield District, South Carolina; September 18, 1793. Her parents were Thomas Mann and Ann Deshazo.

My maternal grand-mother, Ann Deshazo, was born in North Carolina; about the year 1765. Her parents were Robert Deshazo and Mollie Trevelian.

My mother's maternal grand-mother, Mollie Trevelian, was born in Virginia, about the year 1732. One of her parents, I know not which, was born in Scotland, the other in Ireland. When yet young, they migrated from their respective native countries to Virginia, where they married. Later, they moved, with their daughter Mollie and other children, to North Carolina: and there Mollie married Robert Deshazo.

### AN EPISODE.

Mollie Trevelian Deshazo had an elder brother, John Trevelian; who, as a volunteer in the Virginia Militia, participated in the campaign against Fort Du Quesne, in 1755; fought in the battle of Monongahela, — remembered as General Braddock's Defeat, — July 8th, of that year. In that battle, he was captured by the French: and thence he was conducted, a prisoner, to Canada. How long he was held as a prisoner, I am not informed: but he was

finally set at liberty,—pennyless in a strange country, among a
people whose language he did not understand.   There were only
two ways by which he could return home.   One was through a
wilderness, which was infested by savages, who would surely kill
him if he attempted to traverse it alone: and he could not learn of
any body of adventurers whom he could accompany on such a trip.
The other way was to go by sea: but he had not money with which
to pay his passage; and he could obtain employment only for short
terms between intervals, and at low wages.   But he worked when
he could obtain employment at any price; hoping, by rigid economy, to save money enough to pay his way home.   Finally, after
an absence of four or five years, he made the trip home; whether
by land or by sea, I am not informed.   He owned a good home,
which was well furnished for that period; which his friends had
not disposed of, though they believed that he had been killed in
the battle in which he was captured.   He first thought that he
would marry and live on his homestead: but a change of condi-
tions determined him to do otherwise.   He sold his possessions
in Virginia; and went to North Carolina, whither his parents had
already gone.   He never married: but, by industry and economy,
he amassed a fortune.   He was a very pious member of the Methodist Church.   At the beginning of the Revolutionary war, he enlisted in the rebel army, in which he served till the end of the
war.   He resided in North Carolina till he was past ninety years
old.   Then he sold his property; went to South Carolina; and, during the rest of his life, resided with his brother-in-law and sister,
Robert and Mollie Deshazo.   There he orally stated what I have
here said of him to his little grand-niece, Mary Ann Mann: and,
many years later, she, having become my mother, repeated the
same to me.   He died at the residence of Robert Deshazo, in Edgefield District, South Carolina, at the age of ninety-six years.

My mother's maternal grand-father, Robert Deshazo, was born
in Virginia about the year 1730.   He was a son of Nathaniel Deshazo, and grand-son of Peter Deshazo.   Peter and Nathaniel were
born in France.   When Nathaniel was a little boy, Peter came to
America, and settled in Virginia.   There Nathaniel became a
prosperous farmer.   It is evident that Nathaniel's wife was also
born in France, or was totally of French descent: for his son, Rob-

ert, boasted that he was a full-blood Frenchman; though he never learned the French language.

When Robert Deshazo was twenty years old, his father, Nathaniel, wishing to move to a new country, sent him to North Carolina, with money, to purchase land and build a home in that Colony. He found a suitable place; purchased it; and, with hired help, built houses, cleared and inclosed land, and made a crop. He also purchased a fine lot of live-stock. All this he accomplished in one year. Then he returned to Virginia, to move his father's family hither. There being no mails at that time, he had not heard from his family since his departure for North Carolina. Arrived at the old home, he found that his father had died, and his mother and the other children were averse to moving. Therefore his father's heirs amicably effected a partition of the estate; and Robert took, for his part, the property which he had procured and improved in North Carolina. Then he returned to North Carolina, and assumed possession of the home which he had prepared for his parents. This was near the residence of Mr. Trevelian: and, immediately after his return from Virginia, he married Mr. Trevelian's daughter Mollie, and took her to his own home.

Robert Deshazo was an accomplished tobacco-farmer and raiser of live-stock: and, as tobacco then commanded what we, of today, would call fabulous prices, he acquired wealth very rapidly. At the beginning of the Revolutionary war, he owned thirteen negroes, all young Africans, sixteen head of valuable horses, and plenty of other live-stock. He was a pious member of the Baptist Church, highly esteemed by his neighbors: and all his servants loved him, and served him faithfully.

At the beginning of hostilities, Robert's eldest son, Lewis Deshazo, then sixteen years old, enlisted in the regular Continental army; in which he served till the end of the war. But Robert himself stayed at home to care for his family and property: though, whenever there was fighting near him between the Whigs and the Tories, which frequently occurred, he always participated therein, as a volunteer, on the side of the Whigs. But a large majority of his near neighbors were Tories: and this circumstance imperiled his life, and involved the loss of most of his property. At first, his Tory neighbors tried to persuade him to join them: next, they threatened to kill him: and finally, they robbed him of his property, and hunted him as if he were a wild beast. Then he spent much of his time hiding from them in the swamps. After driving away all his horses and cattle, they surprised his negroes in the field, cut off their retreat, and drove away twelve of the thirteen; whom they sold in some distant locality. Only one, a woman named Jinnie, escaped into a swamp. She was a faithful servant; was subjected to several other narrow risks of being captured by the Tories; and at one time, saved her master's life, by warning him of danger: but they never captured her. At another time, they surrounded his dwelling, entered it, cursed his wife, and threatened to kill her unless she would tell them where her husband was: but the heroic Mollie withstood them for hours; and they departed, no wiser for their dastardly conduct.

When the war closed, Robert Deshazo's Tory neighbors, having lost their cause, tried to recover their former friendly relations with him. But they had robbed him, abused his family, and sought to murder him, and offered no restitution: their presence was a torture to him: and he resolved to leave them.

When peace was restored, Robert Deshazo sold his home in North Carolina; and moved to Edgefield District, South Carolina. There he established a new home; and again acquired wealth, but not so rapidly as he had done in North Carolina before the war. Here he and Mrs. Deshazo lived till 1814, when their respective ages were eighty-four and eighty-two years. Then he again sold his home, and made another removal. From Edgefield District, South Carolina, he moved to Twiggs County, Georgia; whither two of his sons had gone, and where they had purchased another home for him. During the next year, 1815, he died, at his home in Twiggs County, Georgia, at the age of eighty-five years. Soon after his death, his wife, Mrs. Mollie Trevelian Deshazo, returned to Edgefield District, South Carolina; and there lived with her daughter, Mrs. Mary Norris, during the rest of her life. She died at the residence of her son-in-law, Nathan Norris, in 1830, at the age of ninety-eight years.

My maternal grand-mother, Ann Deshazo, moved, with her parents, from North Carolina to Edgefield District, South Carolina: and there she married Thomas Mann.

My maternal grand-father, Thomas Mann, was born in North Carolina, about the year 1755. He was a son of John Watts Mann.

My mother's paternal grand-father, John Watts Mann, was born in France: though his parents had been born, brought up and married in Wales. Hence he professed to be "a Welchman born in France." He migrated from France to North Carolina.

My maternal grand-father, Thomas Mann, moved from North Carolina to Edgefield District, South Carolina; and there he married Ann Deshazo, about the year 1792. About the year 1800, my grand-mother, Ann Deshazo Mann, died in her father's house, in Edgefield District, South Carolina, aged about thirty-five years. My grand-father, Thomas Mann, went from Edgefield District, South Carolina, to Florida; where he married again. Later, he moved to Twiggs County, Georgia. Yet later, he moved to Taladega County, Alabama; where he died in 1840, at the age of eighty-five years.

My mother, Mary Ann Mann, was a little girl when her mother died; and was brought up by her maternal grand-parents, Robert and Mollie Deshazo. From them, she learned what I know of her ancestry: and I learned it from her. In 1814 she moved, with her maternal grand-parents, from Edgefield District, South Carolina, to Twiggs County, Georgia. There she continued to live with them till her grand-father's death in 1815. Then she lived with her uncle, William Deshazo, in the same State and County; and was married in his house, to Abraham Zuber jr, February 16, 1816.

My father, Abraham Zuber jr, was born in Lancaster County, Pennsylvania, November 14, 1780. His parents were Abraham Zuber sr, and Mary Bartling.

My paternal grand-mother, Mary Bartling, was born in Denmark; probably between the years 1745 and 1750. Her father was Dr. Bartling, a physician, who always dwelt in cities. From Denmark, he moved to London, England; and, six years later, thence to Philadelphia, Pennsylvania, which was his last residence. He had one son and one daughter, Chrislieb and Mary. (I know not whether he had others or not.) Chrislieb Bartling never moved from Philadelphia. He had two sons, Henry and Charles Bartling, who were ship-masters. About the year 1822, he wrote to his nephew, my father, saying,—"This may be the last letter that I shall ever write: for I am now eighty-two years old."

My paternal grand-mother, Mary Bartling, moved, with her parents, from Denmark to London, England, when she was nine years old; and thence to Philadelphia, Pennsylvania, when she was fifteen years old. In Philadelphia she married Abraham Zuber sr, probably between the years 1761 and 1766.

My paternal grand-father, Abraham Zuber sr, was born in Lancaster County, Pennsylvania, probably between the years 1740 and 1745. His parents were Daniel and Elizabeth Zuber.

I do not know where nor when my father's paternal grand-mother, Elizabeth, was born, nor what her original family name was: but she was of pure German descent, and spoke the German language. She married Daniel Zuber, of Lancaster County, Pennsylvania;—I know not at what date.

My father's paternal grand-father, Daniel Zuber, was a son of German parents; who came from Hanover, Germany, to Lancaster County, Pennsylvania;—whether before or after Daniel's birth, I do not know. Daniel Zuber grew to manhood and died in Lancaster County, Pennsylvania. His grand-son, Daniel Zuber of Georgia, who was my uncle, wrote to me that he was a rebel soldier in the Revolutionary war. I judge that he occupied some easy position: for he had lost a leg, and must have been quite an old man.

My paternal grand-father, Abraham Zuber sr, was of pure German descent; and was brought up among people of like descent, most of whom spoke and wrote only in the German language, and who were called "Pennsylvania Dutch." Such were his parents and their children. He was brought up to speak German, which he called his "mother tongue": though he was educated in both German and English. Soon after reaching his majority, he married Mary Bartling of Philadelphia, and brought her home to Lancaster County. He and his wife used the German as their family language. Both were members of the Lutheran Church: and each had a Lutheran Bible, which they kept and read while they lived.

At the beginning of the Revolutionary war, Abraham Zuber sr, enlisted in the Continental army, in which he served continuously till the close of the war;—excepting that, several times, he was permitted to spend some time at home, with his family, on furlough: and he received an honorable discharge for service during the entire term of the war. I am not definitely informed of the division of the army in which he served: but I infer that, of course, he was among the troops supplied by Pennsylvania. I have been told, in general terms, that he fought in many battles: but, specifically, I am able to mention only one instance in which he was engaged in battle. That was the siege of Yorktown, in 1781.

My paternal grand-father, Abraham Zuber sr, served in the siege of Yorktown, Virginia, under General Washington; and witnessed the surrender of Lord Cornwallis' sword to Washington, October 19, 1781.

If the record of said Abraham Zuber's service was not destroyed by the burning of the capitol in Washington City, by the British army during the war of 1812-1815, it can doubtless be found in the archives of the Department of War. Or, I deem it probable that it may be found in the State archives of Pennsylvania.

In 1786, Abraham Zuber sr, sold his premises in Lancaster County, Pennsylvania; and moved thence to Oglethorpe County, Georgia. There he purchased land, and established a farm, on which he lived during the rest of his life. He and his wife, Mary Bartling, were the parents of thirteen children; twelve of whom lived to manhood or womanhood. About half of these were born in Pennsylvania, the others in Georgia. Those born in Pennsylvania spoke only German while they remained in that State: but, after removal, having no German neighbors in Georgia, they learned to speak English, and abandoned the use of German. Those born in Georgia never learned to speak German.

Abraham Zuber sr died at his home in Oglethorpe County, Georgia, about the year 1802; being probably between fifty-seven and sixty-two years old. Later, when his youngest children had grown up, his widow, Mary Bartling Zuber, abandoned housekeeping, and lived with some of her children. She died at the residence of some one of her children, in Georgia, but I know not in what County, in 1820; probably between seventy and seventy-five years old.

I know not the history of any of the daughters of Abraham

Zuber sr and Mary Bartling. Their sons who were survived by children were Emanuel, Abraham jr, Daniel, John, Jacob, and Joshua.

Emanuel Zuber lived and died in Oglethorpe County, Georgia. He was survived by only one son, Joseph Zuber, who died young, and was survived by one infant daughter.

Of Abraham Zuber jr, I will say more further on.

Daniel Zuber died in Floyd County, Georgia, at the age of seventy-five years. He was the father of thirteen children, all sons; of whom twelve lived to maturity, and eleven became fathers. I know not the history of all of these. One of them, William Moss Zuber, died in Rusk County, Texas; survived by two daughters; Mrs. Martha Ritig, of Minden, Texas, and Mrs. Amanda Hull, of Gary, Texas. Another, Daniel H. Zuber, was, in 1904, Post Master at Kilgore, Texas. Another, B. F. Zuber, resided near Benton, Arkansas, about the year 1880. Another, Joshua Zuber, died in Georgia; but has two daughters near Llano, Texas, who married two brothers of the name of Swanson.

John Zuber died in Lowndes County, Alabama, at the age of seventy-five years; and was survived by two sons and several daughters. One of his sons died unmarried: and the other, Earley Emanuel Zuber, yet lived, unmarried, in 1900, then eighty-two years old, on his own farm, near Grub Gulch, California.

Jacob Zuber died young, leaving an infant son, Jefferson Zuber; who, in 1865, was a farmer near Vicksburg, Mississippi. He had three daughters, all unmarried when I last heard of them.

Joshua Zuber died in Oktibaha County, Mississippi; survived by ten daughters: but I know not whom they married, nor where they now are.

My father, Abraham Zuber jr, was six years old when, with his parents, he moved from Lancaster County, Pennsylvania, to Oglethorpe County, Georgia. He then spoke the German language, which he always mentioned as his "mother tongue." But in Georgia, having no neighbors who spoke German, the children of his parents were necessitated to learn the English language: yet they could not acquire good English while they used the mother tongue; and therefore they abandoned the German: and Abraham jr, being only six years old, totally forgot it.

Reaching his majority, in 1801, my father began to learn the carpenter's trade; not by apprenticeship, but by working at low wages for contractors. As he improved in work, he obtained higher wages: and finally, he became a good workman.

Having worked several years as a carpenter, Abraham Zuber jr became a merchant. He first erected a country store in Putnam County, Georgia, in 1814: but, during the next year, he established a business in the town of Marion, Twiggs County. On February 16, 1816, he married Mary Ann Mann, in that County; who had inherited from her grand-father, Robert Deshazo, a lot of valuable negroes. This enabled him to become a farmer of considerable importance. He accordingly disposed of his store, and purchased a valuable farm, three miles from Marion, and settled upon it.

In 1822, my father sold his farm in Twiggs County, Georgia, and moved to Montgomery County, Alabama: — the part which afterwards became Lowndes County. Thence, in 1824, he moved to East Feliciana Parish, Louisiana; thence, in 1827, to St. Helena Parish, same State; and thence, in 1830, to District of Aes, now San Augustine County, Texas. He had visited Texas in 1827, 1828, and 1829.

In 1831, he moved from District of Aes to Harrisburgh on Buffalo Bayou, in the District of Harrisburgh, now Harris County. Thence, in 1832, he moved to a farm at the east edge of the Brazos bottom, in District of Brazoria, twenty-five miles north of the town of Brazoria. Again, in 1833, he moved from District of Brazoria to his headright league, near the present town of Roan's Prairie, in what afterward became Montgomery County, but the part which is now Grimes County. This was his last residence.

At the organization of Montgomery County, Texas, in 1838, Abraham Zuber was elected its District Clerk: and he served the County as such during some time. During part of his service, his deputy was Dr. Charles B. Stewart, who succeeded him in the office.

Abraham Zuber jr died at his home in Grimes County, Texas, November 24, 1848; aged sixty-eight years and ten days. His wife, Mary Ann Mann Zuber, died near the same place, at the home of her grand-daughter, Mrs. R. B. Gooch, October 20, 1879;

aged eighty-six years, one month and two days. Mr. and Mrs.
Abraham Zuber were members of the Methodist Episcopal Church
South.

Abraham Zuber jr and his wife, Mary Ann Mann, were the
parents of only two children; both of whom survive them. These
were William Physick Zuber and Mary Ann Deshazo Edwards,
nee Zuber.

———

I, William Physick Zuber, was with my parents, Abraham Zuber
jr and Mary Ann Mann, during all their removals; beginning with
their departure from Twiggs County, Georgia, in 1822, when I
was two years old, and ending with their arrival at their last
home, in what is now Grimes County, Texas, in 1833, when I was
in my thirteenth year. I lived with them till past my majority
and was frequently with them as long as they lived. They told me
all of what I have here said of their ancestry and early lives: and
I herein record it for the benefit of my descendants and those of
my sister; that they may know the character of their progenitors;
hoping that they may thereby be inspired with such pride of descent as will induce them to emulate their ancestors in the same
patriotism and other virtues that guided their conduct through
life. Incidental family history is inserted as confirmatory evi-
dence of the main facts.

In my sixteenth year, I enlisted, as a volunteer, in the Texas
Army; in which I served from March 1, 1836, till June 1, 1836;
for which service I received an honorable discharge. This service
was in Capt. James Gillaspie's Company, Col. Sidney Sherman's
Regiment, Texas Army. This was the San Jacinto campaign.
Subsequently, I served on several other campaigns against Mex-
icans and Indians. I also served, *voluntarily*, in Company H,
Twenty-first Regiment, Texas Cavalry, Confederate Army, from
March 20, 1862, till the "break-up" in 1865: during which service
I participated in some hard fighting.

In the spring of 1876, I was elected Justice of the Peace for
Precinct No. 2, Grimes County; which office I filled till the fall
of 1878.

On September 28, 1839, I joined the Methodist Church: and I

am yet, July, 1905, a member of the Methodist Episcopal Church South.

On July 17, 1851, I married Louisa Liles, a very pious Methodist young woman, who had recently come from Missouri: and I lived with her till March 15, 1904, when she died, at the residence of our daughter, Mrs. S. P. Mize, near Iola, Grimes County, Texas; aged seventy-six years. I am now, July, 1905, living at the same place, and with the same daughter. I am now eighty-five years old.

My wife and I were the parents of two sons and one daughter who lived to maturity, married and became parents. These were Daniel Carl Zuber, Rachel Zerena Mize, nee Zuber, and James Andrew Zuber. All my children who lived to maturity were pious members of the Methodist Episcopal Church South: and so continue those who yet live.

My eldest son, Daniel Carl Zuber, became a prominent merchant in Bryan, Texas. He died May 26, 1902. A widow, three daughters and one son survive him. His two elder daughters, Misses Edna and Mabel Zuber, are teachers by-profession. At date of this writing, July, 1905, they are engaged as teachers for the ensuing scholastic year; Miss Edna in the Hillsboro Academy; and Miss Mabel in the Brandon Academy, both in Hill County, Texas. His widow, Mrs. Janie Zuber, nee McDougal, and his two younger children, little Miss Margaret Zuber and Master Neill Daniel Zuber, reside in Bryan, Texas.

My daughter, Rachel Zerena Zuber, married Samuel P. Mize, a landholder and farmer; and lives with him on his farm, near Iola, Grimes County, Texas. She is the mother of three sons and two daughters. Her eldest, a daughter, is Mrs. Ruby McMillan, nee Mize; wife of Walter McMillan, with whom she lives in the City of Austin, Texas. The four others live with their parents. They are Masters Stephen F. Austin-Mize, Alfred Morris Mize, and Bascom Mize, and little Miss Maude Mize.

My younger son, James Andrew Zuber, is a farmer, living on his own land, near Houston Heights, Harris County, Texas. He has one son and three daughters, all yet children. They are Master John Shannon Zuber, and little Misses Willena, Annie and Blanche Zuber.

My sister, Mary Ann Deshazo Zuber, daughter of Abraham Zuber jr and Mary Ann Mann, was born in East Feliciana Parish, Louisiana, April 15, 1826. On April 22, 1847, she married Joseph Rush Edwards, a native of Tennessee, at our father's residence in Grimes County, Texas. After our father's death, she and her husband became the proprietors of his homestead, near the present town of Roan's Prairie, in Grimes County, Texas. She died, at the same place, in 1881, at the age of fifty-five years. Her husband died, at the same place, in 1904, in his eighty-fourth year.

Mary Ann Deshazo Edwards, nee Zuber, was the mother of four sons and three daughters who survived her; all of whom, I believe, yet live, July, 1905. They are, Sarah Cornelia Gooch, nee Edwards, wife of R. Brooks Gooch; address, Granite, Greer County, Oklahoma: William Oscar Edwards; address, Shiro, Grimes County, Texas: Mary Elizabeth Gooch, nee Edwards, wife of Charles M. Gooch; address, Temple, Bell County, Texas: Rev. Warren O. Edwards, Cumberland Presbyterian Preacher; present address, Longview, Anderson County, Texas: Elisha Floyd Edwards; address, Roan's Prairie, Grimes County, Texas: Verginia Mayfield, nee Edwards, wife of Marion Mayfield; address, Shiro, Grimes County, Texas: and Ed Austin Edwards; address, Shiro, Grimes County, Texas.

---

I have prepared the foregoing synopsis of my genealogy and kindred;—hoping that the herein named descendants of my ancestors, and *their* descendants whether yet born or not, may hereby be inspired with an emulation of the virtues of their progenitors. May our Heavenly Father so incline them.

W. P. ZUBER.

www.ingramcontent.com/pod-product-compliance
Lightning Source LLC
Chambersburg PA
CBHW060709280326
41933CB00012B/2368